the weight loss surgery

SLOW COOKER COOKBOOK

60|

quick and easy slow cooker recipes to be enjoyed after weight loss surgery

LASSELLE PRESS CO

LASSELLE PRESS C<u>O</u>

ISBN-13: 978-1911364511
ISBN-10: 1911364510

CONTENTS

VEGETARIAN | 60

SOUPS, SIDES & STOCKS | 69

DESSERTS | 80

DRINKS & SHAKES | 85

INTRODUCTION

INTRODUCTION

Welcome to The Weight Loss Surgery Slow-Cooker Cookbook!

Here at Lasselle Press we understand how confusing and frustrating it can be, both when preparing for weight loss surgery and whilst recovering afterwards.

What can I eat? How much can I eat? What should I avoid? These questions and many more will no doubt be running through your mind - in this book we aim to take away the hard work by providing you with an array of delicious recipes that can be enjoyed after your surgery, using easy-to-find ingredients and simple instructions.

As well as the recipes, we've included an overview of weight loss surgery and the three main types. Additionally, information and advice for pre and post surgery, including diet and lifestyle guidance is also provided. Our shopping and food lists aim to help you stock up your kitchen with essential items, and we hope that the eating out and traveling advice will provide you with the confidence you need to continue socialising and doing the things you love again.

Whether you or someone you know is considering (or has had) weight loss surgery, the good news is that with the right diet and lifestyle, it is more than possible to be healthy and fit and become the best version of yourself. It is always absolutely vital that you use this information alongside professional guidance and consult your doctor before undergoing any dietary or lifestyle changes.

We wish you all the best in the kitchen and in health!

The Lasselle Press Team

C1: WEIGHT LOSS (BARIATRIC) SURGERY OVERVIEW

So Why Get Weight Loss Surgery?

Perhaps you've tried everything to lose weight, possibly most of your adult life, and nothing seems to have worked. Maybe you've developed an emotional relationship with food; one that you turn to when you're feeling down or stressed out. Or it could be that you've struggled with your weight all your life and you just need the support, education and guidance that bariatric surgery offers.

All this being said, weight loss surgery is not the easy way out as many critics might believe. So many people view it in this way, but what they don't realise is that it takes a lifetime of care and healthy choices to maintain weight loss, and that surgery alone is not the answer! Additionally, there is the matter of going through major surgery in itself. This requires a patient to completely adjust their lifestyle and diet both before and after.

That being said, weight loss surgery can provide you with the confidence and mindset you need to be able to lose more weight and keep it off long term. This is because, depending on the type of surgery you have, you will not be able to either consume or absorb as many calories as you did prior to surgery. Furthermore, the education, psychological support and assistance that you will be given, when implemented with dedication, can help change your relationship with food and excess weight forever. This will not only help with healthy weight loss but also work to prevent many other health risks that are associated with obesity.

The Different Types of Weight Loss Surgery

There are three main types of weight loss surgery, each with their own pros and cons. The following information will summarise each procedure, as well as points to take into account when considering which type of surgery is best for you.

1. The Gastric Sleeve

Surgery Time = 1 hour
Hospital Stay = 2 to 3 days
Recovery Time = 2 to 4 weeks

If you have been considering weight loss surgery for a while, you have most likely heard of the gastric sleeve, but what is it exactly? The Gastric Sleeve is a restrictive operation that will make your stomach smaller. This is what helps people lose weight as you will feel full much more quickly. Rather than suffer through starving yourself on a diet, it will help you to make the lifelong necessary change of eating smaller portions.

The gastric sleeve is performed through abdominal incision or by making several smaller incisions and using a camera to guide the surgery. Once the incision has been made, about half or more of your stomach is removed from your body, leaving a tube that is about the size of a banana. This surgery is irreversible.

Why The Gastric Sleeve?

This surgery is best suited for you if:
- You are severely overweight and have tried to lose weight but can't, even with exercise, diet, and medication,
- You have a body mass index of 40 or higher or -
- There is a life-threatening issue that requires you to lose weight.

However, remember that surgery is a tool to help you lose weight - not an instant fix. You will need to eat the right type of foods as well as exercise after your surgery to lose weight and then maintain that weight loss.

What Is The Success Rate?

According to studies, 80% of patients have lost up to 50% of their excess weight after their gastric sleeve surgery and kept it off for at least 5 years. This success rate is based on the patients who followed the eating plan, were physically active, and were realistic about how much weight they needed to lose. Weight loss will take dedication even after the surgery.

What Are The Risks?

After surgery, vitamins and minerals may not be properly absorbed due to the restricted size of the stomach. Other risks during surgery include infection from the incision, a blood clot in the lungs or gall-stones, or a nutritional deficiency such as anemia. That being said there are risks with any type of surgery and these should be weighed up, with a professional, against the potential quality of life post-surgery.

What Are The Benefits?

Gastric Sleeve Surgery:
1. Can help to reduce hunger,
2. Does not involve operating on your intestines,
3. Has a shorter operating time than other weight loss surgeries,
4. Does not require adjustments after surgery,
5. Helps with weight loss over an 18 month period.

How Much Will It Cost?

On average, the cost of the gastric sleeve is around $19,000. Depending on where you are located, it could range from $4,000 to $60,000. It should be noted that this cost will not include your pre-op, post-op, or any complications that may occur. Please note that there are financing options available that will help pay for your surgery if needed.

2. Lap Band Surgery

Surgery Time = Less than 1 hour
Hospital Time = 1 to 2 days
Recovery Time = 10 days

Lap band surgery involves tying an adjustable gastric band around your stomach to make it smaller. It limits the amount of food your stomach can hold. This will help you eat less, become fuller after smaller portions, and ultimately lose weight faster.

This surgery is performed through small abdominal incisions, through which the surgeon will insert a camera to monitor the surgery and tie the band around the upper section of your stomach. The ring around your stomach will be attached to a thin tube that leads to an access port under your skin. This access port will be where your doctor can add and/or take away saline with a needle; the saline is needed to tighten the band to make your stomach smaller. Likewise, the saline will be removed if the ring is too tight.

Why Lap Band Surgery?

This surgery is best suited for you if:
- You are severely overweight and have tried to lose weight but can't, even with exercise, diet, and medication,
- You have a body mass index of 35 or higher or -
- You suffer from a disability due to your weight.

Again, remember that surgery is a tool to help you lose weight - not an instant fix. You will need to eat the right type of foods and exercise after your surgery to lose weight ad then maintain that weight.

What Is The Success Rate?

The success rate is not as high as the gastric band surgery at around 47% of those losing more than 50% of their excess weight and keeping it off for 5 years after the surgery, compared to 80% of gastric sleeve patients.

What Are The Risks?

1.   Access port problems: there is a risk of getting an infection in the access port. The port could also disconnect, leak, or become blocked.
2.   Esophageal dilation: this issue will occur if your band is too tight. It could also happen if you are eating too much. When this happens, your esophagus could expand and make it hard for you to swallow.
3.   Band slippage: for some patients, the band can slip out of place. When this happens, symptoms such as belly ache and heartburn can occur. It is treated by removing fluid in the band. Unfortunately, this could lead to having to have a second operation.
4.   Obstruction: food can sometimes block the opening of the stomach, causing, nausea, pain, or vomiting.
5.   GERD: Another risk of lap band surgery is developing gastroesophageal reflux disease.

What Are The Benefits?

1.   Minimal trauma- the least invasive option,
2.   Fewer risks and side effects,
3.   Adjustable surgery,
4.   Reversible- can be removed at any time,
5.   Effective for long-term weight loss.

How Much Will It Cost?

On average, the cost of a lap band is around $15,000. Depending on your location, it could range between $4,000 and $33,000. This price will vary based on your insurance. There are also other ways to afford the surgery including discounts and other financing options.

3. Gastric Bypass Surgery

Surgery Time = 1.5 hours
Hospital Time = 2 to 3 days
Recovery Time = 2 weeks

Gastric bypass is a procedure that will alter the way your body digests food. The surgery works in two ways: first, it will help with restriction, limiting the amount of food you can consume by reducing stomach size. Second, the surgery will limit the absorption of food by bypassing a section of your small intestine. This combination aids weight loss.

Why Gastric Bypass Surgery?

This surgery is best suited for you if:
- You are at least 100 pounds overweight,
- You have tried to lose weight but can't, even with exercise, diet, and medication,
- You have a body mass index of 40 or higher or -
- You suffer from an obesity related disease.

Once again, remember that surgery is a tool to help you lose weight - not an instant fix. You will need to eat the right type of foods and exercise after your surgery to lose weight and then maintain that weight.

What Is The Success Rate?

The success rate is one of the highest at around 85% losing more than 50% of their excess weight and keeping it off for 5 years after the surgery.

What Are The Risks?

1.   Potential allergic reaction to medication,
2.   Gastritis,
3.   Heartburn or stomach ulcers,
4.   Injury to stomach or other organs during surgery,
5.   Scarring inside stomach,
6.   Vomiting from overeating,
7.   Dumping syndrome- occurs when a lot of food moves in to the stomach too quickly,
8.   Internal bleeding from surgical wounds,
9.   Bowel obstruction.

What Are The Benefits?

1.   Reduces obesity-related illnesses (including diseases such as diabetes, sleep apnoea, and even high blood pressure).
2.   An improved quality of life e.g. a decreased risk of depression and anxiety, improved self-esteem etc.
3.   Long term weight loss - for those who opt for the gastric bypass, they may find that the weight loss post surgery will not only be rapid, but it will also continue over months and years later.
4.   A quick recovery time.

How Much Will It Cost?

On average, the gastric bypass surgery can cost anywhere from $15,000 to $35,000 depending on your location. Again, this price will vary based on your insurance. There are also other ways to afford the surgery including financing options.

C2: YOUR DIET & NUTRITION

As you already know, surgery is not a one stop fix to weight loss; there will be changes you will need to make both before and after your surgery. These changes will be life-long in order to lose your target weight and maintain that weight loss. This chapter will outline key pre and post operation tips.

Pre-Surgery Guidance:

- Eat your meals evenly throughout the day,
- Drink throughout the day- a minimum of 2 liters,
- Do not drink alcohol,
- Take a multivitamin daily (as recommended by your surgeon).

Diet Plan Before Surgery - Recommended Daily Portions Broken Down:

1. Carbohydrates =3 portions
2. Fruit = 2 portions
3. Vegetables = 3-5 portions
4. Protein = 2 portions
5. Milk = 2 portions
6. Keep calories between 800-1000 kcal per day depending on height, weight and surgeon's guidelines.

Serving Size Equivalents

The following lists will help you understand how much is included in a given serving so that you don't go over the recommended serving sizes and portions each day.

Remember that the pre-op diet recommends:

Portions Per Day=
Carbohydrates=3
Protein =2
Fruit =2
Veg = 3-5
Milk = 2

Carbohydrates Example Portion Sizes:

1 Portion =

- 1 medium slice of bread or toast
- 2 small potatoes (boiled or mashed) or 3 petite potatoes with skin
- 5 tablespoons of all-bran
- 2 tablespoons of boiled rice
- 1/2 Weetabix
- 3 tablespoons of boiled pasta
- 2 rich tea biscuits
- 3 tablespoons of bran flakes, fruit & fiber or cornflakes
- 1 digestive biscuit
- 3 tablespoons of dry porridge oats
- 1/2 bagel
- 4 tablespoons of Rice Krispies
- 2 small oat cakes

- 1 crumpet
- 1/2 pita or 1 small pita
2 crisp breads

Proteins Example Portion Sizes:

1 Portion =

- 4 ounces of lean cooked meat
- 2 ounces of low fat soft cheese/low fat cheese/low fat cottage cheese
- 4 ounces of cooked white fish or canned tuna (in spring water or brine)
- 2 medium eggs (maximum of 6 per week) - poached, boiled or scrambled
- 1 small skinless chicken breast
- 4 tablespoons of cooked peas, lentils, beans (including baked beans, kidney beans etc.)
- 4 ounces of tofu or Quorn products

Fruits Example Portion Sizes:

1 Portion =

- 1 medium piece fresh fruit e.g. 1 apple
- 2x small fruits e.g. plums, satsumas
- 5 ounces of strawberries
- 3 tablespoons of stewed or canned fruit (no added sugar)
- 5 fluid ounces of fruit juice (no added sugar)

Vegetables Example Portion Sizes:

1 Portion =

- 3 heaped tablespoons of cooked vegetables e.g. tomatoes (canned or fresh), eggplant, beets, cabbage, spinach, broccoli florets, zucchini, cucumber, fennel, leek, lettuce, watercress, mushrooms, radish, peppers, scallions, rutabaga etc.
- 3 heaped tablespoons of salad
- 1 large tomato or 7 cherry tomatoes
- 6.5 fluid ounces of tomato or vegetable juice (unsweetened)

Dairy Example Portion Sizes:

1 portion =

- 6 1/2 fluid ounces of skim milk
- 1 small pot of non-fat or low-fat yogurt

C3: POST-SURGERY DIET RECOMMENDATIONS & FOOD LISTS

Foods To Enjoy Long Term (After Recovery Stages)

Post-Surgery Guidance

After surgery, you could experience multiple symptoms. These include body aches, dry skin, mood change, hair loss, and feeling tired or cold. These should go away as your body gets used to the weight loss and it will definitely be worth it in the long run!

Depending on the type of surgery you've had as well as a variety of other factors including, age, weight, weight loss goals and recovery stages, your diet will usually begin with clear liquids, progress onto puréed foods, then soft foods and then small portions of 'real' foods. This always needs to be planned with your post-surgery team and/or doctor. The lap band usually has the quickest recovery time, meaning you will likely move on to solids within the shortest period of time after surgery. However this should always be approached slowly and with a professional's guidance.

Portion sizes will be much smaller than what you're used to immediately post surgery:
Liquids -generally recommended portion size = 2-3 fluid ounces.
Purées - generally recommended portion size = 5-6 tablespoons.

Please note that all puréed and solid foods should be introduced gradually. Likewise, the number of portions you can eat will depend on your stage of recovery, the type of surgery you have had, and a variety of other factors. Please always consult with your doctor or post surgery care team to ensure you're following a suitable plan.

General Guidelines - Portion Sizes After Recovery
1 serving =

Food	Amount
Fish	3 Ounces
Chicken/ Meat	3 Ounces
Cooked/Raw Vegetables	½ Cup
Sweet/Baked Potato	1
Cereal	1 Cup
Avocado/ Peanut Butter	1 Ounce/ 2 Tablespoons
Bread	1 Slice
Salad Dressing/ Olive Oil	1 Tablespoon

Meal Size General Guidance-

Each meal should be no larger than the size of your fist.

Grains/ Starches -

Stick with a single serving per day. The grains and starches food group is an excellent source of fiber, energy, B vitamins, minerals, and complex carbohydrates. Stick to whole wheat flour or whole grains including:

-Whole Wheat English Muffins
-Low-fat Saltine Crackers
-Oatmeal
-Cream of Wheat
-Brown Rice
-Soy Crisps

-Melba Toast
-Corn
-Potatoes
-Yams
-Winter Squash

Vegetables -

Vegetables are essential to your diet. This food group will provide vitamin A, vitamin C, energy, and fiber. Aim for at least four servings of vegetables per day including:

-Broccoli florets (not stalks)
-Carrots
-Green Beans
-Asparagus (tips not stalks)
-Spinach
-Peppers
-Mushrooms
-Cauliflower
-Lettuce
-Olives
-Avocado

Fruits -

Include 2 to 3 servings of fruit per day. This will help provide vitamin C, energy, and fiber to your diet. Just be sure to introduce fruits slowly into your diet including:

-Berries
-Bananas
-Kiwi
-Orange
-Peach
-Plums
-Melon
-100% Fruit Juice

Dairy-

Aim for two servings of dairy a day. This will help provide your body with vitamin D and calcium including:

-Skim, Fat-Free, 1% Milk
-Non Fat Yogurt
-Non Fat Cheese
-Non Fat Cottage Cheese
-Eggs

Spices/condiments -

Salt, pepper, fresh or dried herbs, spices, mustard, curry powder, lemon/lime juice, vinegar, yeast extract, fish sauce, soy sauce, Worcester sauce, OXO or other stock cubes, vanilla and other essences.

Healthy Fats (in moderation) including:

-Avocado
-Salmon
-Nuts
-Sardines
-Nut butters
-Coconut oil

Protein Shakes -

While you are recovering from weight loss surgery, protein shakes are a great meal replacement pre and post-operation.

Choose :
-Whey or soy based protein powders
-14g sugar or less per serving.
-5g of fat or less per serving.
-At least 10g of protein per serving.

Add to shakes, yogurt, breakfast oats or cereal **(only if these foods are included in your stage of recovery).**

Potential Problem Foods Post-Surgery

Please note that each patient is unique and foods that may cause problems for one person, may not necessarily cause any issues for another. That being said the following is a list of the foods that seem to cause more problems in general than others. Introducing new foods one by one and keeping a food journal, where you track foods and any symptoms experienced, can really help you identify the foods that do and do not agree with you. Always consult your doctor for specific guidance.

Foods To Avoid Long Term

Vegetables and fruits that contain stringy fibers can be problematic including:

- Fresh Pineapple
- Broccoli Stalks– the stalks may be problematic so cut these off before cooking
- Dried Fruits – can swell inside your body and should be avoided
- Oranges – flesh may be problematic
- Asparagus Stalks
- Rhubarb
- Large Cuts Of Meat – if consuming meat, chop very small and chew thoroughly
- Coconut (difficult to digest)
- Crisps (difficult to digest)
- Soft White Bread (difficult to digest)
- Nuts (such as peanuts, almonds, walnuts) and popcorn may also cause obstructions and are best avoided
- Greasy And Spicy Foods

- Whole Milk
- High Sugar Foods,
- Cakes, Biscuits And Desserts
- High Calorie Drinks (Full Milk, Milkshakes, Alcohol, Fruit Squashes)
- Cereals With Added Sugar
- Fats And Fatty Foods – Butter, Oils, Packaged Snack Foods
- Creamy Soups
- Beef
- Pork
- Shellfish
- Grapes
- Whole Grains
- Corn

Top Tips For Diet & Lifestyle After Your Surgery

1. Only eat three small meals a day,
2. Eat solid foods,
3. Eat slowly and stop eating as soon as you feel full (this may be further up in your chest before the sensation reaches your stomach),
4. Cut your food into very small pieces, then chew each piece as many times as possible before swallowing,
5. Don't overeat (or eat too fast) so as to avoid unpleasant symptoms, such as pain and vomiting,
6. Don't drink during meals. This can flush food out of your stomach pouch and make you feel less full. Avoid drinking fluids 15 minutes before a meal and 45 minutes afterwards,
7. Avoid drinking high-calorie drinks, such as cola, alcohol, sweetened fruit juices and milkshakes. These types of drinks quickly pass out of your stomach and into your small intestine, increasing your calorie intake,
8. Ideally just drink water,
9. You will get most of your calcium requirements from three portions of dairy food each day,
10. Consume 48 to 64 ounces of fluids per day - sip throughout the day and avoid eating and drinking at the same time,
11. Avoid using straws and chewing gum as this might trap air in your pouch causing discomfort and bloating,
12. Remember, your diet is just part of your lifestyle - exercise regime must be implemented and stuck to if you want to keep the weight off. Try to exercise for at least 20 minutes per day. Not only will this help you lose and maintain weight loss, it also comes with a whole host of physical and mental health benefits!

C4: EATING OUT & TRAVELING

Advice For Dining Out:

You don't have to miss out on your favorite restaurants or cuisines for the rest of your life!

Follow these tips to stay healthy and ensure you don't gain back those hard earned weight losses!

1. Look out for small, half portions or side dishes and ask your server for your foods to be cooked without extra salts, butters or sauces.
2. Avoid fried foods and opt for grilled or poached instead.
3. If you know you are going out to eat, plan ahead: look at the restaurant's menu beforehand and decide what you will order to avoid anxiety or stress on the night.
4. Use the food lists in the previous chapter to help you choose and don't feel bad about asking them to cater for your needs.
5. Ensure you have eaten your other meals before you go out for dinner, or time brunch or lunch well so that you can pace out the rest of your meals for the day.
6. Remember to avoid ordering drinks during your meal. Instead you could take it easy after you've eaten and then order a healthy drink.

Advice For Traveling:

Whatever your travel plans, you will have to eat. The following tips should help make this easier for you:

- If you plan ahead, you should be able to make a meal plan to suit your needs.
- If you have a dietitian, tell them where you are going and what you expect to eat at your destination so they can help you with this,
- Remember to pack any multi vitamins you take and continue to take them daily - put a reminder on your phone as it's so easy to forget when traveling, especially across time zones.
- Avoid eating unhealthy snacks by packing healthy options such as fruits, rice crackers and low fat cheeses when you go out for the day,
- You could also take meal replacement drinks to replace a meal when you're out and about and potentially won't be able to find anything suitable.
- If going on a road trip or camping, avoid processed meats. If at all possible, use fresh-cooked meats, low-sodium deli meats, unsalted chicken or tuna.
- Remember to track your calories - apps such as My Fitness Pal allow you to do this on the go. Or do it the old fashioned way and read the labels! Just remember to write it down!
- If you are going on a cruise, all those buffet foods can be tempting to tuck into 24 hours a day. To help with this predicament try to select fresh fruits, salads, and vegetables.
- Remember to include a good source of protein with every meal.
- If you are going to be traveling abroad and don't speak the language, take a phrasebook that has a section for ordering food.

Cooking Tips:

1. Grill, poach, roast or sauté lean meats instead of frying,
2. Steam or boil vegetables instead of frying,
3. Use healthy oils such as extra virgin olive oil instead of butters and vegetable oils.

One Last Thing:

Always remember to only use new recipes and ingredients after speaking to your doctor or dietitian; your needs will be unique to you depending on the type of surgery you underwent as well as how your body has recovered. We hope that with your doctor's advice, along with our guidance and recipes, that you can continue to enjoy cooking, eating and sharing meal times with your love ones as well as losing the weight you set out to lose!

Please note:
It is crucial you see your dietitian to determine the amount of calories you should be consuming each day and adjust the serving sizes according to your individual requirements if necessary.

All nutrition levels have been calculated using The US Department of Agriculture's Super Tracker website www.supertracker.usda.gov and may differ depending on specific brands. It is always advised to track your nutrition using a tracking site such as this one or by studying the individual labels on foods.

We wish you all the best on your weight loss journey.
Happy cooking!

BREAKFAST

All-Ready Oat Porridge

Pop the ingredients into the slow cooker before heading to bed, and wake up to a warm and nutritious breakfast.

1 cup of oats
1 cup of almond milk
1 cup of water
1 teaspoon of ground cinnamon
2 tablespoon of whey/soy protein powder (flavor of your choice)

1/2 cup of raspberries
1 tablespoon of fresh mint, finely chopped

1. Mix the oats, almond milk, water and ground cinnamon into the slow cooker.
2. Set it on LOW and leave it to cook overnight or on HIGH for 1 hour.
3. To serve, add more milk or water if desired. Stir in the protein powder and top with the fresh raspberries and chopped mint.

HINT: Try making your own almond milk. Soak a cup of almonds with water overnight. Discard the water, and blend the almonds with two cups of water. Sieve the almond milk through a muslin cloth. Chill and sweeten if desired.

Per Serving:
Calories: 203
Protein: 11g
Carbohydrates: 31g
Fat: 4g
Sugar: 12g
Sodium: 124mg
Potassium: 277mg
Phosphorus: 187mg
Calcium: 185mg
Fiber: 4g

Delightful Vegetarian Enchiladas

SERVES 2 / PREP TIME: 10 MINUTES / COOK TIME: 2-3 HIGHS ON HIGH

These soft and zingy enchiladas are tasty and filling, served with a burst of vibrant color!

Olive oil cooking spray, for greasing
2 medium corn tortillas
¼ cup of finely chopped yellow bell peppers
¼ cup of finely chopped red bell peppers
¼ cup of finely chopped scallions

½ cup of canned black beans, drained
2 large egg whites
¾ cup of almond milk

1. Lightly grease the base of the slow cooker pot with cooking spray.
2. Lay each tortilla flat on a clean work surface.
3. Mix the yellow bell peppers, red bell peppers, and scallions together. Reserve 3 tablespoons and spoon half the mixture into the center of each tortilla.
4. Now add half the black beans to each.
5. Roll each tortilla into a wrap - fold the outer right side to the center; fold the bottom up to half way; fold the outer left side to the center and roll to tighten.
6. Place the tortillas into the slow cooker pot.
7. Lightly whisk the egg whites with the almond milk and pour gently over the tortillas.
8. Cover with foil, and set the slow cooker on LOW. Cook for four to five hours or until the egg white is set. (If you are short of time, set the slow cooker on HIGH and it will be done in two to three hours.)
9. Remove the foil.
10. To serve, top with the reserved crunchy vegetables and season to taste.

Per Serving:
Calories: 174
Protein: 9g
Carbohydrates: 32g
Fat: 2g
Sugar: 9g
Sodium: 233mg
Potassium: 591mg
Phosphorus: 166mg
Calcium: 282mg
Fiber: 7g

Light & Fluffy Frittata

SERVES 2 / PREP TIME: 5 MINUTES / COOK TIME: 1-2 HOURS ON LOW

Leave the frittata to cook in the slow cooker and come back to a healthy, warm breakfast.

½ red bell pepper, finely diced
¼ cup of green onions, coarsely chopped
½ cup of baby spinach leaves, washed and torn
½ tablespoon of fresh basil, coarsely chopped
4 large egg whites

½ teaspoon of olive oil
freshly ground black pepper, to taste

1. Place the red peppers, green onions, baby spinach leaves, and fresh chopped basil in a large bowl and set aside.
2. Whisk the egg whites with the olive oil and season generously with black pepper.
3. Add the egg whites to the vegetables and mix gently to coat.
4. Pour into the slow cooker and set it to LOW.
5. Let the frittata cook for about an hour or two, until it is set.

Hint: Top the frittata with a low-fat cheese for extra protein.

Per Serving:
Calories: 102
Protein: 12g
Carbohydrates: 10g
Fat: 3g
Sugar: 4g
Sodium: 305mg
Potassium: 576mg
Phosphorus: 67mg
Calcium: 109mg
Fiber: 3g

Delicious Quinoa & Plum Porridge

SERVES 2 / PREP TIME: 10 MINUTES / COOK TIME: 7 HOURS ON LOW

Wake up to the smell of cinnamon-stewed plums in this slow-cooker porridge recipe.

1/4 cup of plums, pitted and sliced
(canned or fresh)
1 teaspoon of ground cinnamon
1 cup of almond milk
½ cup of quinoa
½ cup of fat-free Greek yogurt

---

1. Sprinkle the plums with the ground cinnamon and leave to rest for 10 minutes.
2. Pour the almond milk into the slow cooker pot.
3. Add the quinoa to the almond milk and stir to combine.
4. Add the spiced plums with any released juices to the porridge and mix well.
5. Set the slow cooker to LOW and leave it to cook overnight.
6. Serve hot with ¼ cup of Greek yogurt swirled through each serving.

Hint: Plums are delicious when stewed with a mix of spices such as whole spice powder, star anise, cardamoms, and a little ground nutmeg. Consider whipping up a batch of stewed plums in the slow cooker, and serve alongside meat dishes, or as a dessert with ice cream.

Per Serving:
Protein: 11g
Carbohydrates: 29g
Fat: 3g
Sugar: 10g
Sodium: 86mg
Potassium: 311mg
Phosphorus: 197mg
Calcium: 250mg
Fiber: 3g

Layered Vegetable Frittata

SERVES 2 / PREP TIME: 10 MINUTES / COOK TIME: 5 HOURS ON LOW

Load up on your protein to start the day right, with this tasty vegetable frittata.

½ teaspoon of olive oil
½ cup of cauliflower florets
½ medium carrot, grated
½ cup of finely diced white onion
4 large egg whites

½ cup of almond milk
¼ cup of scallions, chopped
Freshly ground black pepper to taste

---

1. Lightly oil your slow cooker with the olive oil.
2. Layer the slow cooker pot with a third of the cauliflower florets, then a third of the grated carrot, and lastly with a third of the diced onion.
3. Repeat the previous step two more times until all the vegetables are layered.
4. Lightly whisk the egg whites with the milk and scallions. Season generously with black pepper and pour over the vegetables.
5. Set the slow cooker to LOW for 5 hours.

Hint: Cauliflower is low in potassium and high in fiber. You can pulse cauliflower in a food processor into rice, and use it for a low-carb alternative to rice and couscous.

Tip: If you only have a large slow cooker, use a small heatproof oven/casserole dish that fits inside the base of the slow cooker and prepare in exactly the same way.

Per Serving:
Calories: 144
Protein: 12g
Carbohydrates: 18g
Fat: 3g
Sugar: 10g
Sodium: 340mg
Potassium: 531mg
Phosphorus: 77mg
Calcium: 186mg
Fiber: 4g

Chicken Spinach & Red Pepper Omelet

SERVES 2 / PREP TIME: 10 MINUTES / COOK TIME: 2 HOURS ON HIGH

Experiment with different vegetables to add a little variety to your morning.

½ teaspoon of olive oil
5 large egg whites
½ cup of almond milk
4 ounces of cooked skinless chicken breast, sliced
½ a medium red bell pepper, sliced

1. Lightly grease the slow cooker pot with olive oil.
2. Whisk the egg whites with the milk and set aside.
3. Layer half the chicken slices and half the sliced bell peppers in the pot.
4. Pour half the egg mixture over to coat the vegetables.
5. Layer the remaining chicken slices and red pepper and pour over the remaining egg mixture.
6. Set the slow cooker to LOW and cook for 4 hours or 2 hours on HIGH.

Hint: Try serving with a bowl of crunchy cucumber salad dressed with a teaspoon of balsamic vinegar.

Per Serving:
Calories: 188
Protein: 27g
Carbohydrates: 8g
Fat: 5g
Sugar: 7g
Sodium: 580mg
Potassium: 464mg
Phosphorus: 156mg
Calcium: 130mg
Fiber: 1g

Cream of Wheat Goodness

SERVES 4 / PREP TIME: 10 MINUTES / COOK TIME: 7-8 HOURS ON LOW

An old-time favorite; this dish can be tweaked to suit both savory and sweet taste buds just before serving, making it suitable for the whole family!

¾ cup of cream of wheat
1¾ cups of water
2 cups of soy milk (fat free)
1 cup of fat free Greek yogurt
2 tablespoons of chia seeds, milled

1. Place the cream of wheat and water in the slow cooker pot.
2. Set the slow cooker to LOW and cook overnight for 7 to 8 hours.
3. Stir through ¼ cup of Greek yogurt and ½ tablespoon of milled chia seeds to serve.

Hint: For a savory cream of wheat, mix in low-fat cheese like grated cheddar and top with a high fiber vegetable like cabbage or celery.

Per Serving:
Calories: 218
Protein: 14g
Carbohydrates: 34g
Fat: 3g
Sugar: 7g
Sodium: 113mg
Potassium: 286mg
Phosphorus: 258mg
Calcium: 455mg
Fiber: 4g

Hempseed Breakfast Bowl

SERVES 2 / PREP TIME: 5 MINUTES / COOK TIME: NA

This doesn't need the slow cooker but is ready in a flash so simply wake up in the morning, blitz and go!

¼ cup of blueberries
¼ teaspoon of lemon zest
2 teaspoons of hemp seeds
1 teaspoon of chia seeds

2 tablespoons of vanilla flavored protein powder
1 cup of water
½ cup of Greek fat free yogurt

1. Add all ingredients to a food processor and blend until smooth.
2. Serve with extra milled chia seeds on top or a few fresh blueberries.

Per Serving:
Calories: 147
Protein: 17g
Carbohydrates: 16g
Fat: 2g
Sugar: 13g
Sodium: 129mg
Potassium: 275mg
Phosphorus: 177mg
Calcium: 109mg
Fiber: 1g

POULTRY & SEAFOOD

Thyme Turkey with Curly Kale

SERVES 2 / PREP TIME: 10 MINUTES / COOK TIME: 8 HOURS ON LOW

The kale in this dish complements the smoky flavor of the chili.

Olive oil cooking spray
¼ cup of white onion, finely chopped
½ clove of garlic, minced
8 ounces of lean ground turkey
½ teaspoon of smoked paprika

½ teaspoon of dried thyme
¼ cup of low fat chicken broth
½ cup of curly kale, chopped

---

1. Spray a non-stick skillet with cooking spray, and sauté the onions on a medium heat until they become translucent.
2. Add the garlic and ground turkey to the skillet, and continue to sauté until the meat is browned.
3. Remove from the heat and transfer into the slow cooker pot.
4. Mix in the paprika, thyme, and broth.
5. Set the slow cooker to LOW for 8 hours.
6. In the last 15 minutes of cooking, mix in the kale until the leaves are wilted.

Hint: Freeze the leftovers in serving portions. A great way to use serve leftovers is to wrap in fresh, crispy lettuce leaves for a quick and healthy snack.

Per Serving:
Calories: 116
Protein: 13g
Carbohydrates: 5g
Fat: 6g
Sugar: 2g
Sodium: 153mg
Potassium: 476mg
Phosphorus: 92.5mg
Calcium: 37mg
Fiber: 1g

Mild Chicken Curry

SERVES 2 / PREP TIME: 5 MINUTES / COOK TIME: 7-8 HOURS ON LOW

This mild chicken curry can be made a day in advance or the night before, and reheated before serving.

Olive oil cooking spray
¼ cup of white onion, finely chopped
6 ounces of skinless chicken breasts, diced
½ teaspoon of mild curry powder
½ teaspoon of turmeric
½ teaspoon of allspice
½ teaspoon of cumin
½ large carrot, peeled and diced
2 cups of water
1 tablespoon of fresh cilantro, chopped

---

1. Heat the oil in a skillet over medium heat and sauté the onions until they become translucent. Remove from the skillet and set aside.
2. Sear the chicken cubes in the skillet.
3. Return the onions to the skillet, and add in the curry powder, ground turmeric, ground cumin, and allspice powder. Stir to coat the chicken and onions well with the spices.
4. Remove from the heat and transfer into the slow cooker pot.
5. Add the carrots and water to the pot and stir to mix well.
6. Set the slow cooker to HIGH and cook for 4 to 5 hours/7-8 hours on LOW (or until the chicken is cooked through).
7. Serve with a sprinkle of fresh cilantro and salt to taste.

Hint: Serve with cauliflower rice for a low carb side!

Per Serving:
Calories: 164
Protein: 26g
Carbohydrates: 7g
Fat: 4g
Sugar: 2g
Sodium: 436mg
Potassium: 466mg
Phosphorus: 219mg
Calcium: 33mg
Fiber: 2g

Chicken & Summer Squash

SERVES 4 / PREP TIME: 20 MINUTES / COOK TIME: 8 HOURS ON LOW

Delicious for a quick snack!

Olive oil cooking spray
1 cup of onion, finely chopped
2 garlic cloves, minced
9 ounces of skinless chicken breasts, sliced
Freshly ground black pepper, to taste
1 cup of low fat chicken broth
1 cup of water

3 sprigs of fresh thyme
1 bay leaf
½ acorn squash

---

1. Heat the cooking spray in a skillet over medium heat.
2. Sauté the onions and garlic in the skillet until the onions turn translucent (approx. 5 minutes).
3. Now add the chicken and stir until browned. Season with the black pepper.
4. Remove from the heat and transfer the chicken and vegetables into the slow cooker pot.
5. Add the chicken broth, water, fresh thyme and bay leaf to the pot and stir well to combine. Ensure that there is enough liquid to cover the meat and vegetables.
6. Prepare the squash: Cut the squash vertically in half and place on top of the ingredients in the pot (skin-side up).
7. Set the slow cooker to LOW and cook overnight or for 8 hours.
8. Once ready, carefully remove squash from the slow cooker and allow to cool slightly. Use a spoon or fork to scrape out the flesh from the shells and return back to the slow cooker. Stir up and allow to heat through for 10 minutes.
9. Serve and enjoy!

Per Serving:
Calories: 282
Protein: 41g
Carbohydrates: 18g
Fat: 5g
Sugar: 5g
Sodium: 1057mg
Potassium: 944mg
Phosphorus: 367mg
Calcium: 70mg
Fiber: 3g

Turmeric Sweet Orange Chicken

SERVES 2 / PREP TIME: 5 MINUTES / COOK TIME: 8 HOURS ON LOW

A deliciously sweet and tangy recipe.

---

8 ounces of skinless, boneless chicken breast, thickly sliced
1 medium red bell pepper, seeds and pith removed, and finely chopped
1 medium yellow bell pepper, seeds and pith removed, and finely chopped
½ cup of white onion, sliced

1 cup of low fat chicken broth
1 cup of water
2 tablespoons of sweet orange marmalade
1 teaspoon of turmeric

---

1. Combine the chicken, peppers, onions, chicken broth, water, orange marmalade, and turmeric into the slow cooker pot.
2. Set the slow cooker to LOW for 8 hours.

Hint: Double up on ingredients and freeze half the leftovers for another meal for 2 in order to save on preparation time. Simply thaw and heat through completely in the microwave or on the stove top, adding a little extra water if necessary.

Per Serving:
Calories: 315
Protein: 39g
Carbohydrates: 29g
Fat: 6g
Sugar: 11g
Sodium: 591mg
Potassium: 1120mg
Phosphorus: 371mg
Calcium: 53mg
Fiber: 4g

Leek, Fennel & Dill Chicken Stew

SERVES 4 / PREP TIME: 5 MINUTES / COOK TIME: 5-6 HOURS ON LOW

Chicken and leek, infused with the aromatic combination of garlic, dill and fennel seeds.

1 garlic clove, minced
1½ teaspoons of ground fennel seeds
1 teaspoon of dried dill
4 skinless chicken thighs
2 medium leeks, thickly sliced
2 medium carrots, thickly sliced

1 cup of low fat chicken broth
1 cup of water

1. To make the seasoning, combine the minced garlic, ground fennel seeds, and dried dill in a bowl.
2. Score small slashes in the chicken thighs and rub the seasoning on evenly, ensuring you rub into the slashes; set aside.
3. Arrange the leeks and carrots into the base of the slow cooker pot.
4. Pour in the broth and water
5. Arrange the chicken thighs onto the vegetables and set the slow cooker: cook for 2½ to 3 hours on HIGH or 5 to 6 hours on LOW.

Hint: Try lightly toasting the minced garlic, fennel seeds, and dried dill in a non-stick frying pan until aromas are released first. You can then transfer into a mortar and pound until a paste forms. Add just a little oil, store in an airtight container and use for fish, meat and vegetable marinades.

Per Serving:
Calories: 131
Protein: 14g
Carbohydrates: 9g
Fat: 4g
Sugar: 3g
Sodium: 474mg
Potassium: 342mg
Phosphorus: 148mg
Calcium: 48mg
Fiber: 2g

Spanish-Style Chicken

SERVES 4 / PREP TIME: 5 MINUTES / COOK TIME: 7-8 HOURS ON LOW

Delicious for lunch or dinner.

4 skinless chicken thighs
1 cup of onion, roughly chopped
1 garlic clove, minced
1 tablespoon of dried or fresh oregano
1 teaspoon of black peppercorns
1 cup of low fat chicken broth
1 cup of water

½ cup of canned chopped tomatoes (no added salt or sugar)
1 medium red bell pepper, roughly chopped
1 teaspoon of paprika
1 teaspoon of cumin
1 tablespoon of balsamic vinegar

1. Place the chicken thighs, onions, garlic, oregano and black peppercorns in the slow cooker pot.
2. Add the broth, water and tomatoes to the pot and set the slow cooker to HIGH for 7-8 hours or LOW for 3-4 hours.
3. Add the red peppers, paprika, cumin and balsamic vinegar in the last 30 minutes of cooking time.

Hint: Experiment with different herbs and spices in this dish and try adding olives in the last 30 minutes for an extra Spanish feel!

Per Serving:
Calories: 143
Protein: 15g
Carbohydrates: 11g
Fat: 5g
Sugar: 6g
Sodium: 522mg
Potassium: 473mg
Phosphorus: 163mg
Calcium: 54mg
Fiber: 3g

Spiced Caribbean Chicken

SERVES 4 / PREP TIME: 5 MINUTES /COOK TIME: 7-8 HOURS ON LOW

Fragrant spices, juicy turkey and a tangy salsa on the side.

¾ cup of brown rice
¼ cup of canned kidney beans (or dried and soaked overnight)
3 cups of water
1 teaspoon of cumin
1 teaspoon of ground cinnamon
1 teaspoon of dried oregano
1 teaspoon of freshly ground black pepper,

1 garlic clove, minced
4 chicken thighs, skinless and boneless

---

1. Add the rice, kidney beans and water to the slow cooker pot and stir to combine.
2. To make the spice rub: combine the cumin, ground cinnamon, dried oregano, black pepper, and minced garlic.
3. Rub the chicken thighs with the spices and arrange them in the slow cooker pot, nestling under the water as much as possible.
4. Set the slow cooker to LOW and cook for 7-8 hours.
5. Serve with a sprinkling of black pepper to taste.

Hint: Make extra rub and keep in a sealed container somewhere dry to rub onto fishes, poultry and vegetables before cooking.

Per Serving:
Calories: 162
Protein: 15g
Carbohydrates: 15g
Fat: 5g
Sugar: 0g
Sodium: 262mg
Potassium: 220mg
Phosphorus: 174mg
Calcium: 29mg
Fiber: 2g

Turkey & Lemon Risotto

SERVES 4 / PREP TIME: 15 MINUTES / COOK TIME: 6-7 HOURS ON LOW

A delicate blend of flavours - this risotto is deliciously fresh.

Olive oil cooking spray
8 ounces of skinless turkey breasts,
cut into strips
1 cup of brown rice
¼ cup of leek, finely sliced
¼ cup of chopped carrot
¼ cup of chopped red onion
1 cup of low fat chicken broth

½ cup of water
1 teaspoon of dried oregano
1 teaspoon of grated lemon zest
To serve:
Freshly ground black pepper, to taste
Freshly squeezed lemon juice, of ½ lemon
Fresh cilantro, chopped

---

1. Heat 1 spray of cooking oil in a skillet over medium heat.
2. Add the turkey breast slices and stir-fry for 3 to 5 minutes or until the meat is slightly browned.
3. Add the brown rice, leek, carrot, and onion and sauté for 3 to 5 minutes until soft.
4. Remove from the heat and transfer the contents into the slow cooker pot.
5. Pour in the chicken broth and water, and mix through the oregano, lemon zest, and black pepper,
6. Set the slow cooker to LOW and cook for 6-7 hours.
7. Before serving, stir in the black pepper, lemon juice and top with some freshly chopped cilantro.

Hint: Add a little crunch to the dish by serving with garlic flakes. Simply arrange fresh garlic slices in a single layer on a lightly greased oven tray and cook at 150°F until they are dry and slightly darkened in color. Cool before storing in an airtight container and sprinkle on the risotto, salads or soups.

Per Serving:
Calories: 145
Protein: 15g
Carbohydrates: 17g
Fat: 2g
Sugar: 2g
Sodium: 116mg
Potassium: 272mg
Phosphorus: 155mg
Calcium: 29mg
Fiber: 2g

Moroccan-Style Apricot Tagine

An authentic taste without the hard work!

---

2 medium carrots, diced
1 cup of white onion, diced
8 ounces of skinless chicken breasts, diced
½ cup of canned unsweetened apricots, drained and coarsely chopped (not dried)
1 cup of low fat chicken broth

Freshly squeezed lemon juice, of ½ lemon
1 clove of garlic, minced
1 teaspoon of ground cumin
1 teaspoon of ground ginger
1 teaspoon of ground nutmeg
Freshly ground black pepper, to taste
1 cup of green beans

---

1. Place the carrots, onions, chicken and apricots into the slow cooker pot.
2. Whisk together the chicken broth, lemon juice, minced garlic, ground cumin, ground ginger, ground nutmeg and black pepper, and add to the pot.
3. Set the slow cooker for 3½ to 4 hours on HIGH or 6½ to 7 hours on LOW.
4. 15 minutes before serving, add the fresh green beans into the slow cooker and allow to cook through.

Hint: Choose to serve this alone or with flat breads or couscous – just keep an eye on your carbohydrate intake!

Per Serving:
Calories: 169
Protein: 20g
Carbohydrates: 15g
Fat: 3g
Sugar: 6g
Sodium: 374mg
Potassium: 529mg
Phosphorus: 188mg
Calcium: 49mg
Fiber: 3g

Slow Cooker Rice Wine Chicken

SERVES 4 / PREP TIME: 15 MINUTES / COOK TIME: 6-7 HOURS ON LOW

A superior quality of Chinese rice wine like Shaoxing gives a nutty flavor to the chicken dish, while slow cooking removes most of its alcoholic content, creating a healthy and succulent meal.

8 ounces of skinless chicken breast, diced
1 teaspoon of sesame oil
1 teaspoon of low-sodium soy sauce
1 tablespoon of five-spice powder
1 teaspoon of white pepper
1 tablespoon of Chinese rice wine

Olive oil cooking spray
2 garlic cloves, crushed
1 teaspoon of fresh ginger, thinly sliced
1/3 cup of low fat chicken broth
2 cups of snow peas

1. Marinate the chicken pieces with the sesame oil, soy sauce, five-spice powder, white pepper, and rice wine, and set aside.
2. Heat 1 spray of cooking spray in a skillet over medium heat.
3. Add the crushed garlic and ginger slices, and stir-fry lightly until the fragrance is released.
4. Add the chicken to the skillet and continue to stir-fry until the chicken is lightly browned.
5. Remove from the heat and transfer the contents to the slow cooker pot.
6. Add the broth to the pot and set the slow cooker to LOW for 6-7 hours.
7. In the last 10 minutes of cooking time, add the snow peas to the pot.

Hint: Try serving this dish with Chinese noodles. Prepare a bowl of cold water in the sink. Cook noodles in boiling water until al dente then plunge them into cold water to stop the cooking process. To serve, top the chicken and vegetables over the noodles, and sprinkle over a generous amount of freshly chopped Chinese flat-leaf parsley.

Per Serving:
Calories: 167
Protein: 22g
Carbohydrates: 9g
Fat: 4g
Sugar: 4g
Sodium: 510mg
Potassium: 487mg
Phosphorus: 199mg
Calcium: 47mg
Fiber: 3g

Barbecue Pulled Chicken

SERVES 4 / PREP TIME: 10 MINUTES / COOK TIME: 6.5 HOURS ON LOW + 30 MINUTES

Sweet, smoky, melt-in-the-mouth chicken with a hint of spice.

---

1 teaspoon of mustard
2 teaspoons of lemon juice
1 garlic clove, minced
¼ cup of honey
1 tablespoon of tomato ketchup

8 ounces of skinless chicken breast fillets

---

1. To make the marinade: mix the mustard, lemon juice, garlic, honey, and tomato ketchup together in a small bowl.
2. Coat the chicken fillets with the marinade and arrange them in the slow cooker pot, including any excess sauce.
3. Pour over 1/2 cup of water to allow the chicken to steam.
4. Set the slow cooker to LOW for 6 ½ hours.
5. When the cooking time is completed, shred the chicken with two forks, place back in the slow cooker and cook for 30 more minutes.
6. Serve the pulled chicken with your choice of brown bread roll and side salad.

Hint: Make your own ketchup: simply blend a 16-ounce can of tomato paste with a cup of water, an onion, a clove of garlic, half a cup of cider vinegar, two tablespoons of stevia powder, two teaspoons of low-sodium mustard, half a teaspoon of celery seeds, and a quarter teaspoon each of ground cinnamon, ground cloves, dried basil, dried tarragon, and black pepper. Transfer the contents to a large pot, add 3 cups of water and another 12 ounces of tomato paste. Simmer, uncovered but stirring frequently, until thickened and reduced by half. Cool completely before storing in airtight containers.

Please note: nutrition based on pulled chicken dish only.

Per Serving:
Calories: 150
Protein: 21g
Carbohydrates: 10g
Fat: 3g
Sugar: 10g

Sodium: 361mg
Potassium: 281mg
Phosphorus: 165mg
Calcium: 8mg
Fiber: 0g

Roast Chicken & Stuffing

SERVES 10 / PREP TIME: 20 MINUTES / COOK TIME: 4 HOURS ON HIGH

This method of cooking a roast is so simple and easy. Pop it in and wake up to a meal that's already prepared! Simply add the extra sides into the oven before your guests arrive!

½ cup of carrots, coarsely chopped
2 garlic cloves
1 small red onion, quartered
¼ cup of brown breadcrumbs
1 small (approx. 3 pounds) roasting chicken (giblets removed)
Freshly ground black pepper, to taste

1. To prepare the stuffing: blend the carrots, garlic, onions and breadcrumbs in a food processor.
2. Season generously with black pepper, and push the stuffing into the chicken cavity (use washed hands for this and get stuck in!)
3. Place the chicken in the slow cooker pot and set the timer for HIGH and leave for 4 hours or on LOW for 6-7 hours.
4. The chicken will be done when the meat pulls away easily from the bones.
5. Serve with your choice of sides.

Hint: Try shredding chicken and pair with crisp lettuce and bell peppers in a corn tortilla.

Tip: Freeze leftover servings of shredded chicken for quick go-to as a salad topping for lunch.

Per Serving:
Calories: 275
Protein: 18g
Carbohydrates: 7g
Fat: 5.5g
Cholesterol: 0mg
Sodium: 199mg
Potassium: 333mg
Calcium: 2mg
Fiber: 0.5g

Slow-Cooked Chicken in Red Wine Sauce

SERVES 4 / PREP TIME: 10 MINUTES / COOK TIME: 5-6 HOURS ON LOW

Succulent chicken in a rich red-wine sauce.

Olive oil cooking spray
4 chicken thighs, skinless and boneless
1 cup of red wine
2 tablespoons of tomato paste
½ cup of fat free chicken broth
1 cup of diced carrots
½ cup of sliced green onions

½ cup of chopped fresh parsley
2 bay leaves
½ teaspoon of dried thyme

---

1. Heat the cooking spray in a large skillet over medium heat and sear the chicken thighs until lightly browned.
2. Using a pair of kitchen tongs, transfer the chicken to the slow cooker pot.
3. De-glaze the skillet with half a cup of red wine and pour over the chicken.
4. Stir in the remaining wine, tomato paste, and chicken broth.
5. Add the carrots, green onions, parsley, bay leaves, and thyme to the pot, and set the slow cooker to LOW for 5-6 hours.
6. Remove bay leaf before serving.

Per Serving:
Calories: 146
Protein: 14g
Carbohydrates: 7g
Fat: 5g
Cholesterol: 67mg
Sodium: 278mg
Potassium: 447mg
Calcium: 53mg
Fiber: 2g

Chicken & Rice Broth

SERVES 4 / PREP TIME: 5 MINUTES / COOK TIME: 2 HOURS ON HIGH

This is a comforting, chicken broth-based recipe with rice and vegetables.

---

1 cup of dry brown rice
1 cup of fat free chicken broth
2 cups of water
¼ cup of diced carrots
¼ cup of diced leek
¼ cup of diced white onion
2 chicken thighs, skinless and boneless
and diced

---

1. Add rice, chicken broth, water, vegetables and diced chicken to the slow cooker pot.
2. Set the slow cooker to HIGH and cook for 2 hours.

Hint: To cook rice with the slow cooker, use a double portion of water or chicken broth to a portion of rice, and set the slow cooker to HIGH. It should be done in under two hours.

Per Serving:
Calories: 108
Protein: 11g
Carbohydrates: 32g
Fat: 4g
Sugar: 3g
Sodium: 216mg
Potassium: 237mg
Calcium: 25mg
Fiber: 3g

Slow Cooker Lean Turkey Tortillas

SERVES 4 / PREP TIME: 10 MINUTES / COOK TIME: 7 HOURS ON LOW

Fruity and scrumptious.

---

12 ounces of turkey breasts, skinless and boneless
1 cup of canned diced tomatoes (no added salt or sugar)
1 teaspoon of cumin
1 teaspoon of black pepper
4 corn tortillas
½ cup of canned pineapple chunks (unsweetened)
1 cup of romaine lettuce, chopped

2 tablespoons of fresh cilantro, chopped
Lime dressing:
1/4 cup of lime juice,
1 tablespoon of olive oil,
A pinch of sea salt

---

1. Spray slow cooker with cooking spray.
2. Place turkey breasts in the cooker with tomatoes, cumin, and pepper. Stir to combine.
3. Cover and cook on low-heat setting for 7 hours.
4. Prep lime dressing by combining all the dressing ingredients.
5. After 7 hours, shred meat using 2 forks.
6. With a slotted spoon, top each tortilla with 1/4 of the turkey meat.
7. Divide the pineapple among the tortillas.
8. Combine romaine, cilantro, and lime dressing.
9. Top tortillas with the salad and wrap.

Hint: You can double up on ingredients and freeze remaining turkey for up to 1 month in an airtight container. Freeze in portions to ensure you're monitoring your serving sizes.

Per Serving:
Calories: 198
Protein: 20g
Carbohydrates: 20g
Fat: 5g
Sugar: 7g
Sodium: 342mg
Potassium: 465mg
Calcium: 71mg
Fiber: 3g

Slow Cooked Stuffed Peppers

SERVES 2 / PREP TIME: 15 MINUTES / COOK TIME: 6-8 HOURS ON LOW

These stuffed peppers are so easy to cook and can be stuffed with any high protein ingredients of your choice!

2 large bell peppers (any color)
3 ounces of lean ground chicken
¼ cup of dry quinoa
¼ cup of fat free cottage cheese (optional)
1 fresh beef tomato, diced and juices reserved

1 teaspoon of chopped chives
1 teaspoon of chopped fresh parsley
1 teaspoon of dried oregano
½ cup of low fat chicken broth

1. To prepare the bell peppers: cut the tops of the bell peppers off (reserve them), and remove the piths and seeds. Season the cavities with a little pepper.
2. To make the stuffing: mix the remaining ingredients (except chicken broth) in a large bowl until well combined.
3. Pour the chicken broth into the slow cooker pot.
4. Stuff each bell pepper with the stuffing until about three-quarters full and place them upright in the pot. Top them with the reserved bell pepper tops.
5. Set the slow cooker to LOW for 6-8 hours.

Hint: Try amaranth or lentils inside the bell peppers for another protein rich choice.

Per Serving:
Calories: 203
Protein: 14g
Carbohydrates: 26g
Fat: 5g
Sugar: 8g
Sodium: 207mg
Potassium: 731mg
Calcium: 65mg
Fiber: 5g

Slow-Cooked Meatballs with Tomato Sauce

SERVES 4 / PREP TIME: 10 MINUTES / COOK TIME: 2-3 HOURS ON LOW

Tasty low fat meatballs in a rich fresh tomato sauce.

¼ cup of white onion, finely diced
10 ounces of ground chicken
1 tablespoon of chives
1 large egg white
1 tablespoon of tomato paste
1 cup of low fat chicken broth
1 cup of beef tomatoes, finely diced

---

1. Mix the onion, chicken and chives in a food processor until combined.
2. Whisk the egg white in a shallow dish and mix into the meat mixture.
3. Use slightly wet palms to form equal sized meatballs.
4. Mix the tomato paste and chicken broth, and pour into the slow cooker pot.
5. Arrange the meatballs in the pot.
6. Set the slow cooker to LOW for 2-3 hours.
7. With 15 minutes left of cooking time, add the fresh tomatoes, and give the ingredients a good stir.

Hint: Try serving with zucchini spaghetti or cauliflower rice for a low carb alternative to rice or pasta.

Per Serving:
Calories: 117
Protein: 12g
Carbohydrates: 6g
Fat: 5g
Sugar: 3g
Sodium: 147mg
Potassium: 514mg
Calcium: 15mg
Fiber: 1g

Italian Chicken Stew

SERVES 4 / PREP TIME: 10 MINUTES / COOK TIME: 5-6 HOURS ON LOW

Basil and tomatoes pair deliciously with the slow cooked chicken thighs in this recipe.

Olive oil cooking spray
4 chicken thighs (boneless and skinless)
1 medium carrot, peeled and finely diced
½ cup of red onion
1 tablespoon of tomato paste

1 cup of fresh beef tomatoes, quartered
1 cup of low fat chicken broth
1 tablespoon of fresh basil, torn + extra to garnish
A pinch of salt and pepper

1. Heat a large saucepan over medium heat and spray with cooking spray.
2. Add the chicken thighs.
3. Brown the chicken on each side for 3-4 minutes.
4. Remove from the pan and add to the slow cooker.
5. Add the carrot and onions to the slow cooker and stir.
6. Pour over the tomato paste, tomatoes, broth, and basil and mix well to make sure everything is evenly distributed.
7. Season with a little salt and pepper, cover with a lid and cook on low for 5-6 hours.
8. Serve alone or with your choice of petite potatoes or tomato salad.

Per Serving:
Calories: 117
Protein: 12g
Carbohydrates: 6g
Fat: 5g
Sugar: 3g
Sodium: 147mg
Potassium: 514mg
Calcium: 15mg
Fiber: 1g

Slow-Cooked Chicken Thighs with Sweet Potato & Mango

SERVES 4 / PREP TIME: 10 MINUTES / COOK TIME: 7-8 HOURS ON LOW

A wonderful sweet and savory dish.

4 chicken thighs, skinless and boneless
¼ cup of canned mango (unsweetened)
1 sweet potato (yam), peeled and diced
½ cup low fat chicken broth
1 cup of water
1 teaspoon of dried oregano
1 teaspoon of smoked paprika

1. Sear the chicken thighs in a non-stick skillet until browned on each side.
2. Transfer the chicken with its juices into the slow cooker pot.
3. Add the mango and sweet potato to the pot.
4. Add the chicken broth, water, oregano and paprika and set the slow cooker to LOW for 7-8 hours.
5. Serve hot!

Per Serving:
Calories: 126
Protein: 14g
Carbohydrates: 7g
Fat: 4g
Sugar: 2g
Sodium: 253mg
Potassium: 267mg
Calcium: 21mg
Fiber: 1g

Tomato & Green Olive Cod Stew

SERVES 2 / PREP TIME: 5 MINUTES / COOK TIME: 7-8 HOURS ON HIGH

A taste of the Mediterranean!

---

2 x 4 ounce cod fillets
1 bay leaf
2 small potatoes, sliced into 1cm/half-inch thick slices
½ cup of beef tomatoes, chopped
1 cup of water

½ cup of dry white wine
1 tablespoon of fresh parsley, chopped
¼ cup of pitted green olives, whole
A pinch of sea salt

---

1. Combine all ingredients in a slow cooker and cook on LOW for 7-8 hours or HIGH for 3-4 hours until fish is flaky.
2. Flake the cod fillets with a knife and fork and stir.
3. Serve in a deep bowl and enjoy with a side of green vegetables of your choice!

Hint: You can use any sustainable white fish for this dish.

Per Serving:
Calories: 236
Protein: 22g
Carbohydrates: 18g
Fat: 4g
Sugar: 4g
Sodium: 513mg
Potassium: 688mg
Calcium: 44mg
Fiber: 3g

VEGETARIAN

Super Squash Stew

SERVES 4 / PREP TIME: 10 MINUTES / COOK TIME: 6-7 HOURS ON LOW + 30 MINUTES

Low in fat and high in fiber, this dish is packed with vegan friendly protein sources.

---

1 red pepper, diced
1 cup of water
1 teaspoon of ground allspice
1 cup of canned lentils (or dried and soaked overnight)
1 spaghetti squash, sliced in half vertically

---

1. Mix the pepper, water, ground allspice and lentils in the slow cooker pot.
2. Arrange the squash halves, skin side up, on top of the lentil mixture. You may need to cut the squash halves a little so that they fit snugly in the pot.
3. Set the slow cooker to LOW for 6-7 hours.
4. Carefully remove the spaghetti squash halves and use a knife and fork to shred the flesh before placing back into the slow cooker.
5. Stir and cover for a further 30 minutes before serving.

Per Serving:
Calories: 190
Protein: 13g
Carbohydrates: 35g
Fat: 1g
Sugar: 6g
Sodium: 17mg
Potassium: 634mg
Phosphorus: 258mg
Calcium: 49mg
Fiber: 12g

Mediterranean-Stewed Vegetables

SERVES 2 / PREP TIME: 10 MINUTES / COOK TIME: 1-2 HOURS ON LOW

A light dish, rich in flavors and nutrients.

---

2 cups of boiling water
1 cup of sliced zucchini
1 red bell pepper, seeds and piths re-moved, and sliced
1 cup of diced eggplant
1 cup of low fat vegetable broth
1 teaspoon of dried thyme

1 teaspoon of paprika
1 tablespoon of cider vinegar
Freshly ground black pepper, to taste
2 garlic cloves, peeled and crushed
½ cup of artichoke hearts
¼ cup of canned chickpeas, drained
2 cups of fresh organic spinach

---

1. Add all the ingredients into the slow cooker pot (except the spinach).
2. Set the slow cooker to LOW for 1-2 hours.
3. In the last 10 minutes, add the spinach to the top of the ingredients and allow to wilt.

Hint: Top with a swirl of fat free Greek yogurt for an extra boost of protein.

Per Serving:
Calories: 169
Protein: 12g
Carbohydrates: 32g
Fat: 2g
Sugar: 9g
Sodium: 577mg
Potassium: 1412mg
Phosphorus: 231mg
Calcium: 316mg
Fiber: 13g

Slow-Cooked Chunky Root Veggies

SERVES 6 / PREP TIME: 10 MINUTES / COOK TIME 3-4 HOURS ON LOW

Best served steaming hot!

---

1 ½ packets (21 ounces) of soft tofu
1 cup of boiling water
1 small rutabaga, peeled and cubed
2 large carrots, peeled and cubed
2 large turnips, peeled and cubed
1 garlic clove, minced
1 cup of low fat vegetable broth
1 tablespoon of dried rosemary
Freshly ground black pepper, to taste

To serve:
1 tablespoon of fresh parsley, chopped
(optional)

---

1. Add all of the ingredients for the root vegetables to the slow cooker.
2. Set the slow cooker to LOW for 3-4 hours or on HIGH for 1-2 hours.
3. Serve hot with a sprinkling of fresh parsley.

Per Serving:
Calories: 139
Protein: 13g
Carbohydrates: 10g
Fat: 6g
Sugar: 5g
Sodium: 44mg
Potassium: 490mg
Phosphorus: 222mg
Calcium: 345mg
Fiber: 4g

Soft Red Cabbage & Cranberry Sauce

SERVES 5 / PREP TIME: 15 MINUTES / COOK TIME: 1 HOUR ON LOW

Delicious as a side dish, or served steaming hot with a dollop of Greek yogurt.

---

1 cup of red cabbage, shredded
1 tablespoon of canned cranberries, juices drained
1 teaspoon of balsamic vinegar
1 teaspoon of allspice
1 teaspoon of ground black pepper

2 tablespoons of unflavored soy protein powder
2 cups of water

---

1. Place the ingredients in the slow cooker.
2. Set the slow cooker to LOW for 1 hour.

Per Serving:
Calories: 158
Protein: 14g
Carbohydrates: 26g
Fat: 1g
Sugar: 18g
Sodium: 149mg
Potassium: 589mg
Phosphorus: 44mg
Calcium: 105mg
Fiber: 4g

White Cabbage & Lentils with Relish

SERVES 4 / PREP TIME: 5 MINUTES / COOK TIME: 1.5 HOURS ON LOW

This tender slow cooked cabbage is complemented with a cool, crisp relish.

1 medium head of white cabbage, shredded
2 cups of boiling water
Juice from 1 lemon
Freshly ground black pepper, to taste
½ cup of lentils (canned or dried and soaked the night before)

½ small cucumber, diced
1 tablespoon of dried dill
1 cup of fat free Greek yogurt/sour cream

1. Add the cabbage, water and half the lemon juice to the slow cooker pot. Season generously with freshly ground black pepper.
2. Add in enough water until it just covers the cabbage.
3. Add the lentils and stir well.
4. Set the slow cooker to LOW and cook for 1½ hours: the dish is ready when most of the water has been soaked up.
5. While the cabbage is cooking, make the cucumber and dill relish:
6. Mix the cucumbers, dill, remaining lemon juice and Greek yogurt and set aside to chill.
7. Serve the cabbage with the cucumber and dill relish spooned over the top.

Hint: To speed things up -remove the lid of the slow cooker towards the end of the cooking time so that the liquids evaporate faster.

Per Serving:
Calories: 180
Protein: 16g
Carbohydrates: 32g
Fat: 1g
Sugar: 12g
Sodium: 73mg
Potassium: 808mg
Phosphorus: 250mg
Calcium: 197mg
Fiber: 12g

Herby Root Veg & Quinoa

SERVES 4 / PREP TIME: 20 MINUTES / COOK TIME: 5-6 HOURS ON LOW

This is a delicious protein packed stew with quinoa to soak up all the tasty juices.

1 ½ cups of soft tofu, cubed
1 cup of beef tomatoes, roughly chopped
1 tablespoon of mixed dried herbs
2 medium carrots, diced
1 cup of canned pumpkin, diced
1 cup of water
1 cup of quinoa

2 cups of organic spinach

1. Drain and press the tofu 1-2 hours before cooking: simply remove from the package and place on a chopping board. Place another chopping board on the top with something heavy on top of that. The liquids will run out from the tofu. Make sure to place a towel underneath to catch the liquids!
2. Add all the ingredients to the slow cooker and cook on low for 5-6 hours.
3. The quinoa will have soaked up most of the liquid by now and you will be left with a succulent quinoa dish with tender root vegetables.
4. Stir through the spinach, allow to wilt and serve.

Hint: If you're not a fan of tofu, leave it out and replace with the equivalent protein serving of unflavored protein powder mixed through the liquids. Alternatively serve with a high protein green vegetable such as snow peas or broccoli florets.

Per Serving:
Calories: 190
Protein: 13g
Carbohydrates: 27g
Fat: 5g
Sugar: 5g
Sodium: 181mg
Potassium: 909mg
Phosphorus: 271mg
Calcium: 273mg
Fiber: 7g

Roasted Pepper, Spinach & Lime Quinoa

SERVES 4 / PREP TIME: 15 MINUTES / COOK TIME: 3-4 HOURS ON LOW+ 10 MINUTES

Another quinoa dish, this time with a Mexican twist.

---

1 cup of bell peppers (approx. 4 small bell peppers or 2 cut in half)
1 cup of low fat vegetable broth
1 teaspoon of dried oregano
1 teaspoon of ground cumin
¼ teaspoon of smoked paprika
½ cup of canned black beans, drained

¾ cup of uncooked quinoa, rinsed and drained
2 cups of organic spinach
4 fresh lime wedges

---

1. Preheat the broiler to medium heat.
2. To roast the bell peppers, place whole peppers under the broiler for a few minutes until they begin to char.
3. Using a pair of kitchen tongs, rotate the peppers so that their skins are evenly blistered and charred.
4. Remove from the oven and cover loosely with a piece of aluminium foil. This will help the peppers sweat, making it easy to peel off the skins.
5. When cool enough to handle, remove the skins, piths and seeds of the peppers, and cut into slices.
6. Place the vegetable broth, dried oregano, ground cumin, smoked paprika, black beans and bell peppers to the slow cooker pot. Stir.
7. Stir in the quinoa.
8. Set the slow cooker to LOW for 3-4 hours or HIGH for 1-2 hours.
9. Now add the spinach to the slow cooker and wilt for 10 minutes.
10. Serve with a lime wedge.

Per Serving:
Calories: 192
Protein: 10g
Carbohydrates: 32g
Fat: 3g
Sugar: 3g
Sodium: 300mg
Potassium: 775mg
Phosphorus: 267mg
Calcium: 166mg
Fiber: 7g

Greek Rice & Tzatziki

SERVES 5 / PREP TIME: 10 MINUTES / COOK TIME: 2 HOURS ON HIGH

Rice is so simple to prepare in the slow cooker, and adding these delicious Greek ingredients transforms a boring dish to a continental treat!

---

1 cup of dry brown rice
1 cup of low fat vegetable broth
2 cups of boiling water
1 medium green bell pepper, seeds and pith removed, and finely chopped
1 cup of crumbled non-fat feta cheese
½ cup of sliced Kalamata olives
2 cups of organic spinach

For the tzatziki:
2 tablespoons of fresh lemon juice
1 cup of fat free Greek yogurt
¼ small cucumber, diced
1 tablespoon of fresh mint, chopped
1 teaspoon of white wine vinegar
A pinch of sea salt and black pepper

---

1. Add the rice to the slow cooker pot with the broth and water.
2. Set the slow cooker to HIGH for 2 hours or LOW for 4-5 hours.
3. With 30 minutes left of the cooking time, fluff the rice, and mix in the bell peppers, cheese, olives and spinach.
4. Prepare your tzatziki either in advance or when ready to eat: mix all the ingredients for the dip together and season to taste.
5. Serve a portion of the rice with a portion of the dip on top and enjoy.

Hint: Alternatively serve with hummus instead of Tzatziki and a side salad of your choice.

Per Serving:
Calories: 240
Protein: 13g
Carbohydrates: 36g
Fat: 5g
Sugar: 4g
Sodium: 417mg
Potassium: 544mg
Phosphorus: 250mg
Calcium: 255mg
Fiber: 5g

SOUPS, SIDES & STOCKS

Spicy Carrot & Lime Soup

SERVES 2 / PREP TIME: 15 MINUTES / COOK TIME: 7-8 HOURS ON LOW

A lovely heart-warming soup with a little added spice and zest.

---

1 teaspoon of mustard seeds, crushed
1 teaspoon of fennel seeds, crushed
1 tablespoon of ground ginger
4 medium carrots, peeled and chopped
1 cup of diced red onion
1 lime, zest and juice
2 cups of water
1 tablespoon of fresh oregano, chopped
½ cup of fat free Greek yogurt
Freshly ground black pepper, to taste

---

1. Heat a non-stick skillet over medium-high heat.
2. Add the crushed mustard seeds and fennel seeds and stir-fry for a minute.
3. Add the ground ginger and cook for another minute.
4. Add the carrots, onions, and lime juice and cook until the vegetables are softened, about 5 minutes.
5. Remove from the heat and transfer to the slow cooker pot.
6. Add the water, lime zest and juice, and fresh oregano to the pot.
7. Set the slow cooker to LOW for 7-8 hours or HIGH for 3-4 hours.
8. Serve with ¼ cup of Greek yogurt swirled through and black pepper to taste.

Per Serving:
Calories: 184
Protein: 16g
Carbohydrates: 32g
Fat: 1g
Sugar: 15g
Sodium: 156mg
Potassium: 738mg
Phosphorus: 202mg
Calcium: 261mg
Fiber: 7g

Coconut & Lemongrass Turkey Soup

SERVES 5 / PREP TIME: 15 MINUTES / COOK TIME: 4-6 HOURS ON LOW

This recipe uses coconut oil and lemongrass to bring a taste of the Far-East to your dinner table.

---

1 teaspoon of finely sliced lemongrass
1 teaspoon of ground ginger
1 garlic clove, minced
1 tablespoon of fresh cilantro, chopped
1 tablespoon of dried basil
Juice of 1 lime
1 tablespoon of coconut oil
1 cup of diced white onion

12 ounces of skinless turkey breast, diced
½ cup of low fat chicken broth
½ cup of water
1 cup of snow peas

---

1. Crush the lemongrass, ginger, garlic, cilantro, basil, and lime juice in a mortar and pestle to form a paste.
2. Heat the coconut oil in a skillet over medium-high heat and stir-fry the paste for 1 minute.
3. Add the onions and turkey to the skillet and coat evenly with the paste to brown.
4. Add the broth and water, and gently stir.
5. Remove from the heat, and transfer to the slow cooker.
6. Set the slow cooker to LOW for 4-6 hours.
7. Add the snow peas to the soup 15 minutes before the end of the cooking time.
8. Top with scallions and fresh cilantro if desired.

Per Serving:
Calories: 142
Protein: 16g
Carbohydrates: 9g
Fat: 5g
Sugar: 4g
Sodium: 259mg
Potassium: 383mg
Phosphorus: 147mg
Calcium: 49mg
Fiber: 2g

Turkey & White Cabbage Soup

SERVES 2 / PREP TIME: 10 MINUTES / COOK TIME: 7-8 HOURS ON LOW

Slow cooking brings out the sweetness of cabbage in this classic feel-good soup.

Olive oil cooking spray
½ cup of red onion, chopped
1 garlic clove, minced
6 ounces of skinless and lean turkey
breast, diced
½ cup of low fat chicken broth
1 cup of water
½ tablespoon of ground allspice
½ cup of white cabbage, sliced
½ teaspoon of black pepper

---

1. Heat the oil in a skillet over medium heat.
2. Sauté the onions and garlic until fragrant.
3. Add the turkey cubes to the wok and sear until they are lightly browned.
4. Remove from the heat and transfer the ingredients to the slow cooker.
5. Add the broth, water, allspice, and sliced cabbage to the pot.
6. Set the slow cooker to LOW for 7-8 or 4-5 hours on HIGH.
7. Season with black pepper to taste.

Hint: If you're short on preparation time, place the cabbage, broth, water, onions, garlic, and black peppercorns straight into the slow cooker at LOW for the same cooking duration. An hour before done, add turkey meatballs to the soup instead of diced turkey.

Per Serving:
Calories: 135
Protein: 20g
Carbohydrates: 10g
Fat: 2g
Sugar: 4g
Sodium: 123mg
Potassium: 376mg
Phosphorus: 173mg
Calcium: 41mg
Fiber: 2g

Low Fat Vegetable Broth

SERVES 5 CUPS / PREP TIME: 5 MINUTES / COOK TIME: 4-6 HOURS ON LOW

This homemade vegetable broth is low in fat and can be used for many of the recipes in this cookbook.

2 cups of diced onions
1 cup of peeled and diced carrots
3 celery stalks, finely chopped
1 leek, finely sliced
1 garlic clove
1 bay leaf

A handful of fresh herbs of your choice
1 teaspoon of whole black peppercorns
5 cups of water

1. Add all the ingredients to the slow cooker.
2. Set the slow cooker to LOW for 4-6 hours.
3. Strain liquid through a fine-meshed sieve or muslin cloth before use, and discard the vegetables.

Per Serving:
Calories: 73
Protein: 2g
Carbohydrates: 17g
Fat: 0g
Sugar: 7g
Sodium: 59mg
Potassium: 369mg
Phosphorus: 59mg
Calcium: 56mg
Fiber: 24g

Low Fat Chicken Broth

SERVES 10 CUPS / PREP TIME: 10 MINUTES / COOK TIME: 8-10 HOURS ON LOW

Use this homemade broth in many of the recipes in this cookbook, rather than store bought stock cubes for a low fat cooking option.

1 small whole chicken, giblets removed
3 carrots, peeled and chopped
2 medium onions, peeled and chopped
3 stalks of celery, chopped
4 garlic cloves, crushed
2 bay leaves

1 tablespoon of fresh herbs
1 tablespoon of black peppercorns
12 cups of water

1. Place all the ingredients in the slow cooker.
2. Set the slow cooker to LOW for 8-10 hours (overnight).
3. Strain liquid through a fine-meshed sieve or muslin cloth before use, and discard the vegetables.

Hint: You can use leftover vegetables for this recipe.
Freeze in two-cup portions to use with risottos, sauces, and as a soup base for chicken noodle soup.

Per Serving:
Calories: 86
Protein: 6g
Carbohydrates: 8g
Fat: 3g
Sugar: 4g
Sodium: 343mg
Potassium: 252mg
Phosphorus: 65mg
Calcium: 7mg
Fiber: 0g

Mixed Herb Marinade

SERVES 5 / PREP TIME: 5 MINUTES / COOK TIME: NA

A handy dry mix that can be quickly added to olive oil to use as a marinade.

---

1 teaspoon of black pepper
1 garlic clove, minced
2 teaspoon of mustard seeds, crushed
1 teaspoon of dried basil
1 teaspoon of dried thyme
1 teaspoon of dried oregano

---

1. Combine all ingredients in a food processor until a fine powder is formed.
2. Store in an airtight container in a dry place.
3. When ready to use, mix with 1 tablespoon of olive oil and baste meats/fish/vegetables or alternatively use as a dry rub for broiling.

Please note: nutrition based on marinade before oil is added.

Per Serving:
Calories: 7
Protein: 0g
Carbohydrates: 1g
Fat: 0g
Sugar: 0g
Sodium: 1mg
Potassium: 24mg
Phosphorus: 9mg
Calcium: 15mg
Fiber: 0g

Citrus Rice & Beans

SERVES 5 / PREP TIME: 15 MINUTES / COOK TIME: 2 HOURS ON HIGH

This fruity rice pairs well with curries and stews.

---

1 cup of brown rice
1 cup of low fat chicken/vegetable
broth
1 cup of water
¼ cup of mango, diced
½ cup of canned kidney beans, drained

---

1. Add the rice, broth, water, mango, and kidney beans into the slow cooker.
2. Set the slow cooker to HIGH for 2 hours.
3. Serve with a squeeze of lime juice and season with salt and pepper to taste.

Hint: Serve on the side of a high protein dish such as a grilled chicken breast or crunchy tofu.

Per Serving:
Calories: 149
Protein: 5g
Carbohydrates: 29g
Fat: 2g
Sugar: 2g
Sodium: 114mg
Potassium: 181mg
Phosphorus: 117mg
Calcium: 19mg
Fiber: 3g

Mashed Beets

SERVES 4 / PREP TIME: 5 MINUTES / COOK TIME: 6-7 HOURS ON LOW

Vibrant and bursting with goodness, these are a lovely accompaniment to any main dish or salad.

4 whole beets, trimmed and peeled
1 tablespoon of olive oil
⅓ cup of water
1 tablespoon of honey
2 tablespoons of cider vinegar
½ teaspoon of garlic powder
Juice of 1 lemon
Freshly ground pepper, to taste
2 tablespoons of fat free Greek yogurt

1. Combine the beets with the other ingredients and arrange them in the slow cooker pot (reserve the yogurt).
2. Set the slow cooker to LOW until the beets are soft enough to mash.
3. Swirl through the Greek yogurt and mash until smooth.
4. Serve as a delicious snack or with your favorite high protein main dish.

Hint: To make into a purée, blend the cooked beets in a food processor.

Per Serving:
Calories: 79
Protein: 2g
Carbohydrates: 11g
Fat: 4g
Sugar: 9g
Sodium: 43mg
Potassium: 193mg
Phosphorus: 31mg
Calcium: 22mg
Fiber: 1g

Sweet Onion Relish

SERVES 10 / PREP TIME: 5 MINUTES / COOK TIME: 7-8 HOURS ON LOW

A perfect pantry staple! Leave it to cook overnight, and it will be ready to be canned for the pantry before breakfast is over.

2 pounds of medium white onions, peeled and thickly sliced
1 ½ tablespoons of olive oil
1 tablespoon of cider vinegar

1. Place the onions and olive oil into the slow cooker.
2. Set the slow cooker to LOW for 7-8 hours.
3. About an hour left to end of the cooking time, add the cider vinegar to the relish.

Hint: A water bath is an easy method for sealing mason jars. Spoon in the onion relish and tighten the lids. Place the jars in a deep pot and immerse the jars in water. The water level should be about an inch higher than the height of the jars. Set the heat to medium and boil the water to a simmer. Tiny air bubbles will begin to form on the lids of the jars, and the jars are ready when there are no more air bubbles. Remove the jars from the hot water using a jar lifter and cool at room temperature. You can test if the jars are vacuum sealed by tapping on their lids. Sealed jars lids will not rattle when tapped.

Per Serving:
Calories: 87
Protein: 1g
Carbohydrates: 11g
Fat: 5g
Cholesterol: 12mg
Sodium: 4mg
Potassium: 176mg
Phosphorus: 39mg
Calcium: 25mg
Fiber: 1g

Honey & Mustard Glazed Root Veg

SERVES 4 / PREP TIME: 5 MINUTES / COOK TIME: 7-8 HOURS ON LOW

Slow cooked root vegetables with a sweet and savory glaze.

4 medium carrots, peeled and diced
1 small rutabaga, peeled and diced
1 teaspoon of mustard
1 tablespoon of honey
½ cup of water
Freshly ground black pepper, to taste

1. Combine all the ingredients and place them in the slow cooker.
2. Set the slow cooker to LOW for 7-8 hours until the vegetables are tender.
3. Serve with a high protein entrée such as lean turkey breast, tempeh or even just a dollop of fat free Greek yogurt.

Per Serving:
Calories: 66
Protein: 2g
Carbohydrates: 16g
Fat: 0g
Sugar: 11g
Sodium: 57mg
Potassium: 394mg
Phosphorus: 64mg
Calcium: 57mg
Fiber: 3g

DESSERTS

Strawberry & Peach Crumble

SERVES 4 / PREP TIME: 10 MINUTES / COOK TIME: 6-7 HOURS ON LOW

A perfect dessert for every season!

---

2 cups of sliced strawberries
2 cups of sliced peaches
1 tablespoon of grated lemon zest
1 cup of gluten-free oats
1 tablespoon of chia seeds, milled
½ teaspoon of ground cinnamon

---

1. Mix the strawberries, peaches and lemon zest, and place them in the slow cooker.
2. Mix the oats with the milled chia seeds and ground cinnamon, and top over the fruits.
3. Set the slow cooker to HIGH for 2-3 hours or on LOW for 6-7 hours.
4. The crumble is ready when the fruits are bubbling and the topping turns golden brown.

Per Serving:
Calories: 138
Protein: 4g
Carbohydrates: 26g
Fat: 3g
Sugar: 8g
Sodium: 3mg
Potassium: 296mg
Phosphorus: 142mg
Calcium: 52mg
Fiber: 6g

Sugar-free Applesauce

SERVES 10 / PREP TIME: 5 MINUTES / COOK TIME: 1 HOUR ON HIGH

Try making this simple homemade applesauce as an accompaniment to meats, fish and vegetables or even porridge.

8 large apples, peeled, cored and diced
2 cups of water
¼ lemon, juice of
1 teaspoon of ground cinnamon

1. Add all the ingredients into the slow cooker.
2. Set the slow cooker to HIGH for 1 hour.
3. Stir a couple of times during the cooking time.
4. Mash the stewed apples with a fork for a chunkier applesauce, or blend them for a smooth applesauce.

Hint: Applesauce can be used to substitute oil for baking moist cake and pancakes. A quarter cup of applesauce can also be used to substitute an egg for many baking recipes.

Per Serving (1/2 Cup):
Calories: 66
Protein: 0.5g
Carbohydrates: 15g
Fat: 0g
Sugar: 11g
Sodium: 1mg
Potassium: 116mg
Phosphorus: 12mg
Calcium: 9.5mg
Fiber: 2.5g

Easy Rice Pudding

SERVES 4 / PREP TIME: 5 MINUTES / COOK TIME: 2.5 HOURS ON HIGH

A winter warmer!

---

1 cup of cooked brown rice
1 teaspoon of vanilla extract
2 cups of rice/almond milk
Raw honey, to taste
¼ cup of cranberries

---

1. Stir together the rice, vanilla extract, and rice milk into the slow cooker pot.
2. Set the slow cooker on HIGH for 2 ½ hours or LOW for 4-5 hours.
3. To serve, stir in a little honey and top with cranberries.

Per Serving (1/2 Cup):
Calories: 106
Protein: 2g
Carbohydrates: 20g
Fat: 2g
Sugar: 8g
Sodium: 80mg
Potassium: 89mg
Phosphorus: 51mg
Calcium: 236mg
Fiber: 2g

Poached Spiced Apples & Pears

SERVES 4 / PREP TIME: 5 MINUTES / COOK TIME: 7-8 HOURS ON LOW
Sweet and fragrantly spiced for a delicious dessert.

---

2 apples, peeled and halved
2 pears, peeled and halved
1 tablespoon of cloves
1 teaspoon of allspice
1 cinnamon stick

---

1. Turn the slow cooker to a low setting.
2. Peel and half the apples and pears.
3. Poke the cloves into the flesh of the fruits evenly.
4. Place into the slow cooker and cover with water.
5. Add the allspice and cinnamon stick. Mix.
6. Cover and cook for about 7-8 hours.
7. Remove the cinnamon stick before serving. The juices will have caramelized and formed a delicious sauce to serve with the fruits. Add fat-free Greek yogurt if desired.

Per Serving:
Calories: 84
Protein: 1g
Carbohydrates: 23g
Fat: 0g
Sugar: 15g
Sodium: 2mg
Potassium: 175mg
Phosphorus: 18mg
Calcium: 15mg
Fiber: 4g

DRINKS & SHAKES

Immune Booster Shake

SERVES 1 / PREP TIME: 5 MINUTES / COOK TIME: NA

Try this blend to boost your immune system and fight off the common cold!

1/4 cup of fresh spinach
1/4 lemon with rind
1/4 lime with rind

1/2 orange
1 teaspoon of honey
2 cups of water
1 teaspoon of freshly ground ginger

1. Blend all ingredients in a food processor.
2. Serve over ice and enjoy.

Per Serving:
Calories: 106
Protein: 2g
Carbohydrates: 20g
Fat: 2g
Sugar: 8g
Sodium: 80mg
Potassium: 89mg
Phosphorus: 51mg
Calcium: 236mg
Fiber: 2g

Leafy Protein Smoothie

SERVES 2 / PREP TIME: 5 MINUTES / COOK TIME: NA

No need to add protein powder, the ingredients in this smoothie are packed with protein.

1/4 cup of kale
1/4 cup of raspberries
1/4 cup of sliced mango

1 tablespoon of almond butter (unsweet-ened)
2 cups of almond milk

1. Blend all ingredients in a food processor.
2. Serve over ice and enjoy.

Per Serving:
Calories: 167
Protein: 3g
Carbohydrates: 23g
Fat: 7g
Sugar: 19g
Sodium: 176mg
Potassium: 281mg
Phosphorus: 75mg
Calcium: 507mg
Fiber: 3g

Chia Berry Boost

SERVES 2 / PREP TIME: 5 MINUTES / COOK TIME: NA

A great meal swap or something to keep you going between meals.

1/4 cup of spring greens
1/4 cup of blueberries
1 tablespoon of chia seeds

2 cups of water

---

1. Blend all ingredients in a food processor.
2. Serve over ice and enjoy.

Per Serving:
Calories: 46
Protein: 1g
Carbohydrates: 6g
Fat: 2g
Sugar: 2g
Sodium: 3mg
Potassium: 63mg
Phosphorus: 65mg
Calcium: 49mg
Fiber: 3g

Carrot & Ginger Smoothie

SERVES 2 / PREP TIME: 5 MINUTES / COOK TIME: NA

Ginger is great for stomachs and carrots are packed with Vitamin A - excellent for eye sight !

1/4 carrot, peeled
1 teaspoon of raw honey
1/4 cup of apple, cored and de-seeded
1 teaspoon of freshly ground ginger
2 cups of water

1. Blend all ingredients in a food processor.
2. Serve over ice and enjoy.

Per Serving:
Calories: 24
Protein: 0g
Carbohydrates: 6g
Fat: 0g
Sugar: 5g
Sodium: 6mg
Potassium: 53mg
Phosphorus: 6mg
Calcium: 5mg
Fiber: 1g

Homemade Tomato Juice

SERVES 2 / PREP TIME: 5 MINUTES / COOK TIME: NA

Nutrient packed and a great pick-me-up.

1/4 cup of spinach
1/4 cup of chopped beef tomatoes
1/4 lime with rind
1/2 teaspoon of black pepper

1/4 teaspoon of Worcestershire sauce (optional)
1/4 teaspoon of Tabasco (optional)

1. Blend all ingredients in a food processor.
2. Serve over ice and enjoy.

Per Serving:
Calories: 8
Protein: 0g
Carbohydrates: 2g
Fat: 0g
Sugar: 1g
Sodium: 4mg
Potassium: 86mg
Phosphorus: 9mg
Calcium: 10mg
Fiber: 1g

Marvellous Mango Shake

SERVES 2 / PREP TIME: 5 MINUTES / COOK TIME: NA

Delicious tropical juice drink

1/4 cup of spinach
1/4 cup of sliced mango
1 teaspoon of flax seeds
2 cups of water/fruit juice

---

1. Blend all ingredients in a food processor.
2. Serve over ice and enjoy.

Per Serving:
Calories: 25
Protein: 1g
Carbohydrates: 4g
Fat: 1g
Sugar: 3g
Sodium: 4mg
Potassium: 74mg
Phosphorus: 19mg
Calcium: 12mg
Fiber: 1g

Peach Iced-Tea

SERVES 2 / PREP TIME: 15 MINUTES / COOK TIME: NA

Ditch the latte for this energizing drink!

---

1 tablespoon of loose black or green
tea leaves
1 cup of canned peaches, sliced
1 lemon

---

1. Boil a pot of water and add the peach slices.
2. Simmer for 10 minutes before turning off the heat.
3. Add the loose tea leaves and allow to steep for 5-7 minutes.
4. Pour liquid through a sieve or tea strainer.
5. Enjoy hot with a wedge of lemon for squeezing.

Per Serving:
Calories: 90
Protein: 1g
Carbohydrates: 24g
Fat: 0g
Sugar: 17g
Sodium: 11mg
Potassium: 188mg
Phosphorus: 19mg
Calcium: 11mg
Fiber: 2g

Super Green Shake

SERVES 2 / PREP TIME: 5 MINUTES / COOK TIME: NA

Kick start your day with a delicious green shake!

1/4 cup of Swiss chards
1/4 cup of sliced pear
1/4 cup of sliced apple, cored and de-
seeded
2 cups of water
1 teaspoon of honey (if desired)

---

1. Blend all ingredients in a food processor.
2. Serve over ice and enjoy.

Per Serving:
Calories: 30
Protein: 0g
Carbohydrates: 8g
Fat: 0g
Sugar: 6g
Sodium: 10mg
Potassium: 57mg
Phosphorus: 6mg
Calcium: 5mg
Fiber: 1g

Apple & Banana Smoothie

SERVES 2 / PREP TIME: 5 MINUTES / COOK TIME: NA

Zesty and refreshing!

1/4 cup of spinach/kale
1 ripe banana
1/4 cup of sliced apple, cored and de-
seeded
2 cups of water

---

1. Blend all ingredients in a food processor.
2. Serve over ice and enjoy.

Per Serving:
Calories: 61
Protein: 1g
Carbohydrates: 16g
Fat: 0g
Sugar: 9g
Sodium: 4mg
Potassium: 247mg
Phosphorus: 16mg
Calcium: 7mg
Fiber: 2g

Banana & Nut Butter Shake

SERVES32 / PREP TIME: 5 MINUTES / COOK TIME: NA

Yum!

1/4 cup of spinach
1 ripe banana, peeled
1 teaspoon of almond/cashew butter
2 cups of cashew/almond milk

---

1. Blend all ingredients in a food processor.
2. Serve over ice and enjoy.

Per Serving:
Calories: 91
Protein: 1g
Carbohydrates: 16g
Fat: 3g
Sugar: 13g
Sodium: 109mg
Potassium: 179mg
Phosphorus: 28mg
Calcium: 317mg
Fiber: 1g

CONVERSION TABLES

Volume

Imperial	Metric
1 tbsp	15ml
2 fl oz	55 ml
3 fl oz	75 ml
5 fl oz (¼ pint)	150 ml
10 fl oz (½ pint)	275 ml
1 pint	570 ml
1 ¼ pints	725 ml
1 ¾ pints	1 liter
2 pints	1.2 liters
2½ pints	1.5 liters
4 pints	2.25 liters

Oven temperatures

Gas Mark	Fahrenheit	Celsius
1/4	225	110
1/2	250	130
1	275	140
2	300	150
3	325	170
4	350	180
5	375	190
6	400	200
7	425	220
8	450	230
9	475	240

Weight

Imperial	Metric
½ oz	10 g
¾ oz	20 g
1 oz	25 g
1½ oz	40 g
2 oz	50 g
2½ oz	60 g
3 oz	75 g
4 oz	110 g
4½ oz	125 g
5 oz	150 g
6 oz	175 g
7 oz	200 g
8 oz	225 g
9 oz	250 g
10 oz	275 g
12 oz	350 g

REFERENCES

American Society for Metabolic and Bariatric Surgery. 2016. Bariatric Surgery Procedures - ASMBS. [ONLINE] Available at: https://asmbs.org/patients/bariatric-surgery-procedures. [Accessed 01 December 2016].

Bariatric Surgery Source. 2016. Gastric Sleeve Surgery - All You Need to Know - Bariatric Surgery Source. [ONLINE] Available at: http://www.bariatric-surgery-source.com/gastric-sleeve-surgery.html. [Accessed 14 July 2016].

Bon Voyage after Weight Loss Surgery | . 2016. Bon Voyage after Weight Loss Surgery | . [ONLINE] Available at: http://www.gulfcoastbariatrics.com/weight-loss-surgery-blog/bon-voyage-after-weight-loss-surgery. [Accessed 01 December 2016].

Bray, G.A. (2012) 'Diet and exercise for weight loss', JAMA, 307(24). doi: 10.1001/jama.2012.7263.

Dining Out Tips - UCLA Bariatric Surgery, Los Angeles, CA. 2016. Dining Out Tips - UCLA Bariatric Surgery, Los Angeles, CA. [ONLINE] Available at: http://surgery.ucla.edu/bariatrics-dining-out-tips. [Accessed 01 December 2016].

Francini-Pesenti, F., Brocadello, F., Vettor, R., Bernante, P. and Foletto, M. (2009) 'P-80: Very low or low calory diet before bariatric surgery?', Surgery for Obesity and Related Diseases, 5(3), p. S51. doi: 10.1016/j.soard.2009.03.148

Gastric Bypass (Malabsorptive) Surgery Procedure | Johns Hopkins Medicine Health Library . 2016. Gastric Bypass (Malabsorptive) Surgery Procedure | Johns Hopkins Medicine Health Library . [ONLINE] Available at: http://www.hopkinsmedicine.org/healthlibrary/test_procedures/gastroenterology/gastric_bypass_malabsorptive_surgery_procedure_92,p07988/. [Accessed 14 July 2016].

Gastric bypass surgery: MedlinePlus Medical Encyclopedia. 2016. Gastric bypass surgery:

MedlinePlus Medical Encyclopedia. [ONLINE] Available at: https://medlineplus.gov/ency/article/007199.htm. [Accessed 14 July 2016].

Gastric Sleeve Surgery - Qualifications & Complications | UPMC . 2016. Gastric Sleeve Surgery - Qualifications & Complications | UPMC . [ONLINE] Available at: http://www.upmc.com/Services/bariatrics/approach/surgery-options/Pages/gastric-sleeve.aspx. [Accessed 14 July 2016].

Grocery Shopping after Bariatric Surgery. 2016. Grocery Shopping after Bariatric Surgery. [ONLINE] Available at: http://www.bmiut.com/grocery-shopping-after-bariatric-surgery/. [Accessed 01 December 2016].

Harbottle, L. (2011) 'Audit of nutritional and dietary outcomes of bariatric surgery patients', Obesity Reviews, 12(3), pp. 198–204. doi: 10.1111/j.1467-789x.2010.00737.x.

Heekoung Youn, M.S. (2015) 'Clinical efficacy of a medical-ly supervised low-calorie diet program versus a conventional carbohydrate-restricted diet', Journal of Obesity & Weight Loss Therapy, 05(03). doi: 10.4172/2165-7904.1000267.

How It Works | The LAP-BAND® System. 2016. How It Works | The LAP-BAND® System. [ONLINE] Available at: http://www.lapband.com/r_lapband_about_how. [Accessed 14 July 2016].
Bariatric Surgery Source. 2016. Lap Band Surgery - All You Need to Know - Bariatric Surgery Source. [ONLINE] Available at: http://www.bariatric-surgery-source.com/lap-band-bariatric-surgery.html. [Accessed 14 July 2016].

Keith, C., Goss, L., Blackledge, C., Stahl, R. and Grams, J. (2016) 'Insurance-mandated Pre-Operative diet and outcomes following Bariatric surgery', Surgery for Obesity and Related Diseases, 12(7), pp. S31–S32. doi: 10.1016/j.soard.2016.08.075.

Lifestyle Changes That Come With Bariatric Surgery | University of

Utah Health Care. 2016. Lifestyle Changes That Come With Bariatric Surgery | University of Utah Health Care. [ONLINE] Available at: http://healthcare.utah.edu/bariatricsurgery/lifestyle-changes.php. [Accessed 01 December 2016].

Obesity Coverage. 2016. Gastric Sleeve Surgery - The Expert's Guide. [ONLINE] Available at: http://www.obesitycoverage.com/gastric-sleeve-reference-manual/. [Accessed 01 June 2016].

Obesity Coverage. 2016. The Big Gastric Sleeve Diet Guide. [ONLINE] Available at: http://www.obesity-coverage.com/the-big-gastric-sleeve-diet-guide/. [Accessed 01 December 2016].

(2014) Pre-Op liquid diet. Available at: http://www.murfreesborosurgical.com/weight-loss-surgery/pre-op-liquid-diet/ (Accessed: 28 February 2016).

Pre Bariatric Surgery Diet by Pacific Bariatric. 2016. Pre Bariatric Surgery Diet by Pacific Bariatric. [ONLINE] Available at: http://www.pacificbariatric.com/pre-bariatric-surgery-diet. [Accessed 01 December 2016].

(2014) Pre-Op liquid diet. Available at: http://www.murfreesborosurgical.com/weight-loss-surgery/pre-op-liquid-diet/ (Accessed: 27 March20176.

WebMD. 2016. Gastric Sleeve Surgery. [ONLINE] Available at: http://www.webmd.com/diet/obesity/restrictive-operations-stomach-stapling-or-gastric-banding. [Accessed 05 June 2016].

Weight loss surgery - Life after surgery - NHS Choices. 2016. Weight loss surgery - Life after surgery - NHS Choices. [ONLINE] Available at: http://www.nhs.uk/Conditions/weight-loss-surgery/Pages/Recommendations.aspx. [Accessed 01 December 2016].
2017, wlsinfo (2017) Home › WLS Info. Available at: http://www.wlsinfo.org.uk (Accessed: 27 February 2017).

INDEX

Made in the USA
Coppell, TX
12 October 2024

38562259R10059